Goal Setting

B. Vincent

Published by RWG Publishing, 2021.

While every precaution has been taken in the preparation of this book, the publisher assumes no responsibility for errors or omissions, or for damages resulting from the use of the information contained herein.

GOAL SETTING

First edition. July 16, 2021.

Written by B. Vincent.

Also by B. Vincent

Bookkeeping
Bridge Pages
Business Acquisition
Business Bogging
Marketing Automation
Better Meetings
Conversion Optimization
Creative Solutions
Employee Recruitment
Startup Capital
Employee Mentoring
Followership
Servant Leadership
Human Resources
Team Building
Freelancing
Funnel Building
Geo Targeting
Goal Setting
Immanent List Building
Lead Generation
Leadership Course
Leadership Transition
LinkedIn Ads
LinkedIn Marketing
Messenger Marketing
New Management
Newsfeed Ads
Search Ads

Goal Setting

When talking about objectives, Jim Rohn once said, it's impossible to tell what you can do when you get enlivened by them. Who knows what you can do when you have confidence in them. Furthermore, it's impossible to tell what will happen when you follow up on them. Furthermore, Zig Ziglar reveals to us an objective appropriately set is most of the way reached and there right? Nothing drives us forward like having an alluring objectives that are before us. That is valid for the two people just as for associations. Having that picture in our brain of a future state or an achievement gives us the inspiration we need to keep on track, useful and viable. Also, on a hierarchical level objectives give a feeling of clearness that keeps everybody in total agreement and gives your colleagues a reasonable feeling of mission. However, how would we execute objective setting most successfully? How would we move toward this such that allows us the most elevated opportunity of really accomplishing our objectives, both in our associations and in our own lives? In this course, we're demonstrating how to do precisely that.

93% of representatives can't attach their activities to hierarchical objectives. 37% of representatives feel dicey about their working environments vision or procedure. 32% of representatives need to keep tabs on their development they've made toward objectives set by their supervisors. These insights show that objective setting is an undeniably significant region that organizations should zero in on. Our course will comprise of a progression of basic conversation focuses. These are intended to cover this expansive subject as altogether as conceivable to empower development in these indispensable regions. Also, to work with a genuine and productive conversation inside your association about how you can each develop this fundamental trademark, both at work and in your own lives as a rule. A portion of these will be quite long, and some will be somewhat direct and brief. At the finish of this guide, comes the main last advance. Conversation time, don't avoid this progression. This is the main piece of this preparation. At the point when you finish this course, you need to go through no less than an hour or so going over the inquiries we supply toward the finish of the gathering. Whoever's the big enchilada in the gathering should assign a facilitator whose duty it is that each question is covered, and that everybody time allowing, can express their opinion, ensure all commitments are esteemed, all ideas considered, and all assessments regarded.

So how about we move into the primary conversation point. Pick objectives that spur you. With regards to objective setting, you need to ensure that every objective you make persuades you. This implies that you exceptionally esteem every objective and accomplishing them has a genuine reason. Nonetheless, in the event that you have objectives that you have next to no intrigue in or feel to be excessively insignificant according to your viewpoint, you most likely will not place in the work to accomplish them. Keep in mind, inspiration is the way to accomplishing objectives. To ensure that every objective is persuasive. You should know the why. For what reason is it significant? For what reason does it should be accomplished? You can likewise ask yourself, if I somehow happened to impart this objective to my group, how might I demonstrate to them that accomplishing this objective would be advantageous. Utilizing persuasive worth articulations assist you with keeping away from sensations of uncertainty or vulnerability that an objective can be accomplished. All things considered, it gives you the drive to continue put forward explicit objectives. Suppose you request a pizza on the telephone. In the event that you give out hazy directions on where you reside, the odds of you eating a hot pizza will be pretty much nothing. Additionally, laying out ambiguous indistinct objectives will not lead you to your ideal result. Or on the other hand far and away more terrible, it would be a misuse of your time, energy, and assets. objectives that are explicit or clear and obvious. It ought to figure out what you need to accomplish and how you need it to wind up. This is particularly obvious with regards to your organization's vision. A summed up viewpoint will not characterize what should be finished. explicit objectives give substance, giving you clearness on what you need to achieve. Defining objectives that are quantifiable objectives ought to be quantifiable, or as such, ought to be not difficult to monitor objectives that are engageable assist you with evaluating your present advance and decide your level of achievement. For instance, if your objective is just characterized as to diminish costs of doing business, how might you realize when you've accomplished your objective? Indeed, how might you even know whether you're really gaining ground?

To lay out quantifiable objectives, you should initially distinguish the actual metric. Then, at that point set a particular number you're attempting to meet or surpass. Separating your objectives to scaled down achievements help you screen your advance and remind you to praise each little success. isolating your objectives in explicit measurements likewise holds you back from getting overpowered. All things considered, it inspires you to be constant, and keep up with your energy. Make objectives that are achievable. Each time you put out objectives, you need to ensure that everything's reachable. This implies that objectives ought not be crazy to such an extent that it is difficult to accomplish. All things considered, our goals ought to be plausible and commonsense to accomplish. Making an objective that you realize you will not have the option to accomplish will just discourage yourself and hose your certainty. Notwithstanding, try not to define objectives that are excessively simple. accomplishing something that you put little exertion into is useless and wasteful. Moreover, whenever you've become acclimated to accomplishing such easy objectives, you'll begin to foster a dread of defining objectives that convey a danger of non accomplishment. All things being equal, make objectives that are feasible yet testing. This assists you with raising the stakes each time you put out an objective. In addition, it gives you incredible fulfillment each time you accomplish one. Make your objectives pertinent. Regardless of whether it's an individual or business objective, significance ought to be the fundamental concern. These are objectives that make a difference to you. Furthermore, it likewise lines up with other pertinent objectives. To ensure you have significant objectives you need to glance first in your general vision. Then, at that point partition your vision with progressive objectives.

Then, at that point ask yourself, does my present objective fit my general vision? Does it orchestrate with my different objectives? These inquiries will assist you with inspecting if your objective merits seeking after. Your objectives ought to likewise fill in as venturing stones to the organization's prosperity. This implies that your more modest objectives can make building blocks that assist you with accomplishing bigger ones, accordingly making consistency towards your ideal result. Then again, diffused and conflicting objectives will just squander your time and energy. put forward time touchy objectives. Napoleon Hill portrayed it best when he said an objective is a fantasy with a cutoff time. All objectives ought to have a due date forced on it. This is to guarantee that work completes on schedule and gives you the inspiration to remain on track and accomplish it's anything but a cutoff time, then, at that point your objective would be nothing worth in excess of a fantasy. Chipping away at time delicate objectives builds your desire to move quickly and pushes you as far as possible. It might require arduous exertion from you, yet the fulfillment of accomplishing such objectives is precious. Record it Dr. Gayle Matthews from the Dominican University of California studied 267 individuals and discovered that you were 42% bound to accomplish your objectives on the off chance that you record them. For what reason is that so? It influences you mentally. Actually recording your objectives gives substantial quality gives you an unmistakable image of what you need to achieve. The way toward recording objectives on paper improves your psychological abilities by constraining you to plan, survey your advancement, and consistently conceptualize groundbreaking thoughts on the best way to accomplish them. Seeing your objectives recorded consistently fills in as an every day update for you to continue to push ahead. Make an activity plan. winging your direction to an objective is a major no. You need to make a strong activity intend to arrive at an objective Tragically, this progression has regularly been ignored. A few group are so centered around the result that they neglect to design every one of the means expected to accomplish that objective. Truth be told, some even defined objectives without realizing how to accomplish them. Here are the segments of an activity plan. A distinct depiction of the objective to be accomplished.

Blueprint of assignments that should be completed individuals who will be accountable for doing each undertaking achievements cutoff times. assets expected to finish each job and measures to assess progress. Having an activity plan gives an unmistakable course of how you need to accomplish every objective. It assists you with remaining submitted all through each task. Additionally, activity plans urge you to focus on assignments dependent on exertion and effect. Put out authoritative objectives, hierarchical objectives or targets deliberately intended to work on the construction of a business and friends overall. It diagrams the expected outcomes and guides representatives endeavors. Laying out explicit authoritative objectives assists the organization with keeping tabs on its development and figure out which regions they need to zero in on. hierarchical objectives ought to consistently resound with your representatives having a reasonable comprehension of the organization's targets and empowers them to decide their strategy on the best way to add to accomplishing them. As a business, you should ensure that your workers are furnished with the fitting apparatuses and assets expected to meet these authoritative objectives. Laying out authoritative objectives additionally supports the working environment resolve for a joins representatives to work intently in accomplishing a solitary ultimate objective. This working environment congruity will most likely bring about a more elevated level of proficiency, and efficiency. assist workers with recognizing position explicit objectives. As chiefs, you may have characterized assumptions for every representative, except it shouldn't generally be the situation. All things considered, toward the day's end, they know themselves better than you do. What you can do is request that your representatives recognize objectives that are explicitly connected with their positions. At the point when administrators perceive how their objectives fit with the organization's targets, they should then rapidly assist them with creating activity intends to accomplish those objectives. Jobs shift in the working environment.

Be that as it may, objectives similar to usefulness and productivity are frequently extremely successful. As you work with your representatives, make it a highlight lessen blunders and lift efficiency. This thusly, will save additional time, produce more deals, and further develop your prosperity. Keep away from rivalry. accomplishing objectives can now and then be misinterpreted as a type of rivalry, particularly for representatives who have comparative jobs and duties. Whenever left untreated, this can cause interior competitions and will ultimately bring down work environment confidence. To forestall this, directors should lay out predictable objectives that urge representatives to fill in collectively as opposed to being rivals. These objectives should assist them With supplementing each other, so they can work in an amicable style. Put forward objectives lined up with the organization's goals. Each objective should connect to the organization's qualities and its general development technique. You need to assist your representatives with seeing how their individual jobs can have an extraordinary effect on hierarchical development. At the point when they handle things according to the organization's perspective, it assists them with getting more engaged and inspired to accomplish their objectives. This thusly will add to the headway of the business and increment worker execution. Award representatives who arrived at their objectives. As things get going, directors can here and there neglect to recognize the difficult work of our steadfast representatives. Truth be told, they may be devoured such a huge amount in their work that they neglect to recall the individuals who have at last arrived at their objectives. At the point when such endeavors go unseen, they will begin to feel that nobody esteems their work, and may even lead them to search for a task elsewhere. Try not to allow one more day to pass by without offering acknowledgment to your workers. Set aside effort to survey the advancement of every one, and laud them for their endeavors. Indeed, even a basic thank you for your diligent effort is sufficient to cause them to remain alert.

Each time a representative arrives at an objective, make certain to give them the acknowledgment that they merit. This can be a type of a prize, reward testament, or even only a public affirmation in your next staff meeting. Showing your appreciation praises the workers endeavors. Besides, this is a decent method to show the group that your organization esteems such responsibility and difficult work. This thus will inspire others to try sincerely so they can arrive at their objectives as well. Backing workers who miss the mark. Not every person has a similar speed. Some rapidly dominate in their field. While some actually battle to discover their qualities. supervisors ought to rush to help such ones. For example, suppose that a representative neglects to convey upon the concurred cutoff time and objectives weren't met. Rather than rapidly communicating your failure. Why not have a one on one discussion and examine momentarily what turned out badly. Then, at that point consistently finish strong by urging them to put in more effort and address the issue right away.

Set up B witches. In the book worked to last fruitful propensities for visionary organizations, Jim Collins and Jerry porras. first authored the term Big Hairy Audacious Goal or B witch. As per Collins and timberlands, a B witch is their drawn out objective that is lined up with your organization's basic beliefs and reason. In any case, contrasted with other long haul objectives, B witches are strong, bold aspirations that may nearly appear to be difficult to accomplish, yet it tends to be finished. There are four sorts of B witches good example, intended to mirror other effective organizations. Target situated has a characterized quantitative or subjective objective. shared adversary conceived to contend with top organizations in your industry and inward change centers around the organization's change. B witches are intended to invigorate individuals by allowing them to consider some fresh possibilities, propel themselves out of their usual ranges of familiarity and fortify the work environment cooperative energy. V witches invigorate progress inside your organization and makes a big difference for the force. It's anything but a convincing objective that an association ought to make progress toward. Most likely an incredible illustration of a b witch is the renowned presentation of President Kennedy in 1961. This country ought to concede to accomplish the objective before this decade is out of handling a man on the moon and returning him securely to Earth. This obviously turned into a reality when the principal fruitful moon landing was made in 1969. b witches invigorate individuals in the business, however they appeal to the general population also. Consider space goes about for instance. Their objective of empowering human investigation and settlement of Mars got into public consideration. However they didn't spellbind individuals for having an over the top thought. But since they're demonstrating to the world that life on Mars is, indeed, conceivable.

What makes a decent B witch? Here are the key components. It's 50 to 70% attainable should be clear and convincing. pushes the organization's ability is quantifiable, lined up with the association's methodology. Also, in a perfect world 10 to 25 years in length.

How would you make a B witch for your organization? Here are three basic advances. conceptualize, think about a fresh thought. Try not to be hesitant to reach skyward test measure if it's truly worth devoting to for the following 10 or more years. Submit, work on it right away. Separate it by making achievements. Gracious, grounded B witch joins the organization with one clear reason and vision. It's anything but a major impact on current and future enrollment. For you are resolved to choose the perfect individuals that can transform this vision into a reality and it likewise draws in the opportune individuals to Furthermore, be witches assist with transforming an organization into a superb visionary for what's to come.

Direct a SWOT investigation. A SWOT examination is a remarkable vital procedure that assists an association with surveying its business. The essential target of SWOT is to assist organizations with fostering a full attention to the inner and outside factors that can influence a business choice. A SWOT examination should be done before objective laying out to guarantee that the objectives you set commendation the necessities of the organization. Here's the breakdown of SWOT qualities. What are we acceptable at? shortcomings? What regions do we have to further develop openings? What prospects are coming up for us? what's more, dangers? What can possibly hurt the association? a SWOT examination is advantageous for it's a wellspring of data for key arranging. It perceives center qualities, switches the shortcomings, amplifies openings, and dodges authoritative dangers. By evaluating past and current exhibitions, it assists the organization with chalking up its arrangements for what's to come. Monitor your advancement. How might you know whether your new eating regimen plan works on the off chance that you don't check your weight? Exactly the same thing applies to objective setting. You can possibly know whether you're gaining ground in case you're keeping in track with your objectives. Indeed, monitoring your advancement is exceptionally valuable and intellectually invigorating. As you finish an achievement, take a gander at your advancement. What changes have you taken note? As you measure your action consistently, you will see enhancements. Commend each little success and utilize this as inspiration to work more enthusiastically. stay submitted. Defining objectives isn't only a simple commitment for your business. Objective setting is a continuous cycle. That is the reason a significant degree of responsibility is required. All things considered objectives aren't accomplished for the time being. You must place in the work and develop self-restraint. Continuously ensure that the significance worth and need of every objective remaining parts consistent as time passes by. incorporate monetary objectives. Obviously, in contrast to any organization, monetary objectives ought to be one of the fundamental goals of your association. A healthy monetary objective can be raising $10,000 for a worthy mission by giving 5% of benefits from each deal or expanding deals by 20% to forestall cutbacks. At the point when you routinely speak with your group about your monetary objectives, and how the organization apportions it's anything but, a decent possibility that they would regard the monetary objective as their own objective when representatives see how arriving at the objective would profit them and the organization, they will be all the more persevering, realizing that they've contributed something for a decent purpose.

Deal with your time shrewdly. Using time effectively is fundamental on the off chance that you need to accomplish your objectives. At the point when you deal with your time shrewdly, you will complete each achievement on time, and arrive at each objective immediately. Other than focusing on, you can deal with your time by molding yourself intellectually. Peter Bergman, a top of the line writer promoted a book entitled 18 minutes, which discusses discovering your concentration so you can complete the right things. By utilizing 18 minutes of your time every day, you can battle interruptions and gain efficiency. Here's the means by which 18 minutes all summarizes. Morning, five minutes. Start the day by considering how can be dealt with accomplish your objective today. then, at that point take those things off your plan for the day and timetable them into your schedule. minute each work hour, eight minutes. as you approach your eight to five work. You need to pull together yourself. set a caution each hour. Each time the caution goes off. think about what have you done the previous hour. Ask yourself, have I spent the last hour accomplishing something useful? evening, five minutes. After you've killed your PC, pause for a minute to contemplate. Take a full breath and recap how your day went. Another approach to ensure you're utilizing your time admirably is by taking out interruptions in the work environment. Our telephones can be a genuine danger for accomplishing objectives. You will not see that you've gone through three hours of your day simply checking your telephone when you can do is to set your telephone to a setting that you realize you will not be annoyed. A few group even mood killer their telephones when required. Another great tip is conceal these interruptions from you. You can do this by placing it's anything but a spot past your range. This can be the base piece of your cabinet or inside the most profound pockets of your sack. Additionally ensure that your work region is helpful for usefulness. close any tabs with respect to web-based media, web based shopping, or whatever other stages that can entice you to await your opportunity. focus on your objectives. objectives have various requirements. So you need to focus on appropriately. Try not to skip objectives. bouncing starting with one objective then onto the next won't just burn through your time, yet it will likewise keep you from completing anything. You can focus on assignments adequately by utilizing the A B C D E technique promoted by Brian Tracy. The A B C D E technique permits you to check the degree of significance for every objective. So you can focus on them as indicated by its direness. Here's the means by which the ABCDE strategy works. A vital these are the MIT's most significant errands of your business or association. These errands ought to be your most noteworthy need for it would be the premise of accomplishment for the business. be significant. These are undertakings that are important also, just less significantly. Such undertakings will prompt minor adverse results when disregarded. It's obvious, ideal to do. These things are the ones that have no outcomes by any means. If you do them. D representative these are undertakings that you can relegate to somebody generally my rethinking II dispense with. These are illusionary to levy that are truly, really garbage. You ought to dispose of these ASAP.

Utilize an objective following programming. We can't generally monitor all that we do. We're not robots. However, this cutting edge period of tech can assist us with doing as such. Luckily, we're currently experiencing a daily reality such that everything includes mechanization these advancements Geez help a ton of organizations to save additional time, cut down costs and increment productivity, we ought to expand the utilization of such present day instruments. There are various objective following programming's that a ton of entrepreneurs and workers use to make objectives and keep tabs on their development. Here are some broadly utilized stages trackstar week done 15 five, engagingly, Asana, grid and JIRA. Utilizing a gold following programming assists directors with following their objectives, yet it likewise evaluates worker execution. Likewise, as representatives see their improvement, it propels them to work considerably harder. utilizing programming likewise decreases your pressure, assisting you with taking each objective in turn. Set KPIs. A key exhibition marker or KPI is a measurement esteem that demonstrates how successfully an organization is in accomplishing its business destinations. KPIs help to assess the achievement of arriving at their objectives. Here's the means by which to make a KPI. Compose an unmistakable goal. Your KPI ought to be fundamental to the business. It needs to communicate something vital about the thing your business is attempting to do. Offer it with your workers, correspondence is central. Your representatives need to comprehend the objectives according to your viewpoint and how their assistance can add to the accomplishment of the organization. survey them intermittently. monitor your KPIs every once in a while. This is crucial for keep tabs on your development and survey the organization's turn of events. You can do this on a week after week or month to month premise. Ensure it's significant. Gap KPIs to make present moment and long haul objectives. Adjust to fit evolving needs. Associations adjust to new practices alter KPIs to supplement new changes. Update goals when required. Organizations develop and KPIs ought to routinely verify whether KPIs are should have been changed or rejected right away. At the point when organizations use KPIs, it joins representatives to run after shared objectives. data gathered from KPIs can likewise help in creating future methodologies for the business. Make transient objectives. transient objectives are some laid out objectives that an organization can accomplish more than a little while or a couple of months. These objectives fill in as venturing stones to accomplish long haul objectives. Moreover, accomplishing transient objectives makes an energy of development. In the event that you have a private venture, here are some commonsense instances of transient objectives that can assist with focusing on deals and promoting. Pay attention to client input, robotize regulatory errands, build up client connections and conceptualizing thoughts on the most proficient method to contend with different enterprises. momentary objectives make quantifiable achievement, for you can consider its to be as they occur. Having short time periods, it's anything but a need to keep moving for the group that supports the degree of inspiration. As you accomplish a transient objective, it builds your prosperity pace of accomplishing your drawn out objectives.

Lay preparation for long haul objectives, long haul objectives or targets planned for what's to come. This requires a broad measure of time and cautious arranging. These generally range between three to five years, and can even outfit to 10 years to accomplish. as business people your drawn out objectives ought to reflect for the development of the business, yet your own advantages also. Here are some useful instances of long haul objectives that you can set. increment deals, extend to new freedoms increment brand acknowledgment Create an enduring heritage or notoriety, and host special occasions. long haul objectives provide you an unmistakable guidance of where your business is going. It gives the group a feeling of direction of having something extraordinary to anticipate. Additionally, it assists us with seeing the master plan of what's available for the business. Accomplishing long haul objectives makes an enduring effect that adds to better progress. What's more, presently, it's conversation time. The main piece of this preparation whoever's the big enchilada in the gathering should assign a facilitator whose duty it is that every one of the inquiries you see on your screen is covered and that everybody time allowing, can give their opinion, ensure all commitments are esteemed. All ideas considered and all suppositions regarded.

Don't miss out!

Visit the website below and you can sign up to receive emails whenever B. Vincent publishes a new book. There's no charge and no obligation.

https://books2read.com/r/B-A-QWUO-NYMQB

BOOKS 2 READ

Connecting independent readers to independent writers.

Also by B. Vincent

Affiliate Marketing
Affiliate Marketing
Affiliate Marketing

Standalone
Business Employee Discipline
Affiliate Recruiting
Business Layoffs & Firings
Business and Entrepreneur Guide
Business Remote Workforce
Career Transition
Project Management
Precision Targeting
Professional Development
Strategic Planning
Content Marketing
Imminent List Building
Getting Past GateKeepers
Banner Ads

Bookkeeping
Bridge Pages
Business Acquisition
Business Bogging
Marketing Automation
Better Meetings
Conversion Optimization
Creative Solutions
Employee Recruitment
Startup Capital
Employee Mentoring
Followership
Servant Leadership
Human Resources
Team Building
Freelancing
Funnel Building
Geo Targeting
Goal Setting
Immanent List Building
Lead Generation
Leadership Course
Leadership Transition
LinkedIn Ads
LinkedIn Marketing
Messenger Marketing
New Management
Newsfeed Ads
Search Ads

About the Publisher

Accepting manuscripts in the most categories. We love to help people get their words available to the world.

Revival Waves of Glory focus is to provide more options to be published. We do traditional paperbacks, hardcovers, audio books and ebooks all over the world. A traditional royalty-based publisher that offers self-publishing options, Revival Waves provides a very author friendly and transparent publishing process, with President Bill Vincent involved in the full process of your book. Send us your manuscript and we will contact you as soon as possible.

Contact: Bill Vincent at rwgpublishing@yahoo.com www.rwgpublishing.com